Network and Information Systems (NIS) Regulations

A pocket guide for operators of essential services

Network and Information Systems (NIS) Regulations

A pocket guide for operators of essential services

ALAN CALDER

IT Governance Publishing

IT Governance Publishing Ltd
Unit 3, Clive Court
Bartholomew's Walk
Cambridgeshire Business Park
Ely, Cambridgeshire
CB7 4EA
United Kingdom
www.itgovernancepublishing.co.uk

© Alan Calder 2018

The author has asserted the rights of the author under the Copyright, Designs and Patents Act, 1988, to be identified as the author of this work.

First published in the United Kingdom in 2018 by IT Governance Publishing.

ISBN 978-1-78778-052-1

ABOUT THE AUTHOR

Alan Calder is the founder and executive chairman of IT Governance Ltd (*www.itgovernance.co.uk*), an information, advice and consultancy firm that helps company boards tackle IT governance, risk management, compliance and information security issues. Alan is an acknowledged international cyber security guru and a leading author on information security and IT governance issues. He has many years of senior management experience in the private and public sectors.

CONTENTS

INTRODUCTION

Technology has brought us into a world that many of us only poorly understand. While we may have some grasp of this technology, there is often a lack of real understanding as to how these technologies work and interact. A few decades ago, we understood that if the water levels fell then the hydroelectric plant would not be able to generate electricity. We knew that interchanges connected our phones to other phones elsewhere in the world. We had some appreciation of the fact that supermarkets and other retailers would have to call suppliers and wholesalers in order to have food delivered. Essential services and infrastructure were quite simple to understand.

Nowadays, so much has been automated and interlinked that it can be difficult to understand how our phone calls are connected or where our power comes from. Most people do not need to really understand how society continues to function. They do not need to know that RFID chips attached to crates of fruit make sure there is always fresh fruit on supermarket shelves. The electricity grid is driven by hundreds of power stations, with the flow managed, surpluses stored and shortfalls accounted for automatically. Our phones connect to remote cell towers and flicker between them to maintain the best possible connection. For the most part, as long as everything keeps working, we have no desire to understand any of this.

What we do want, however, is reassurance that these services will not be interrupted. This is not just for the benefit of the common person: our whole society relies on critical infrastructure, and this infrastructure is supported by a set of services. In the modern world, these services and infrastructure can be attacked not just physically but also digitally, and digital attacks can have significant repercussions in the physical world.

In 2014, a German steel factory suffered a cyber attack that caused significant physical damage to its machinery by turning off industrial controls.[1] More famously, the original Stuxnet worm infected the Natanz nuclear facility in Iran in 2010 and destroyed almost one-fifth of the country's nuclear centrifuges.[2] In 2015, Ukraine was the victim of what is believed to be the first successful attack against a power grid, which left 230,000 people without power for up to six hours.[3]

Unfortunately, cyber criminals need to find just *one* weakness to infiltrate and potentially cause damage, but an organisation has to patch *all* of its vulnerabilities and defend against *all* types of attacks. These threats are significant not just because they are difficult to stop but also because they are increasingly within reach of even common criminals. Only a few years ago, a Polish teenager was able to hack into the tram network in Lodz, derailing several carriages and injuring 12 people[4]; you might have reasonably assumed that such attacks came from state actors or well-funded terrorist or dissident groups, but it is the

---

[1] SANS ICS, "German Steel Mill Cyber Attack", December 2014, *https://ics.sans.org/media/ICS-CPPE-case-Study-2-German-Steelworks_Facility.pdf*. For more information, see: Bundesamt für Sicherheit in der Informationstechnik, "APT-Angriff auf Industrieanlagen in Deutschland", *Die Lage der IT-Sicherheit in Deutschland 2014*, 2014, *www.bsi.bund.de/SharedDocs/Downloads/DE/BSI/Publikationen/Lage berichte/Lagebericht2014.pdf*.

[2] William J. Broad, John Markoff and David E. Sanger, "Israeli Test on Worm Called Crucial in Iran Nuclear Delay", *New York Times*, January 2011, *www.nytimes.com/2011/01/16/world/middleeast/16stuxnet.html*.

[3] Kim Zetter, "Inside the Cunning, Unprecedented Hack of Ukraine's Power Grid", *Wired*, March 2016, *www.wired.com/2016/03/inside-cunning-unprecedented-hack-ukraines-power-grid/*.

[4] John Leydon, "Polish teen derails tram after hacking train network", *The Register*, January 2008, *www.theregister.co.uk/2008/01/11/tram_hack/*.

nature of information to be replicated and reused. As such, the threat is proliferating and will continue to do so.

In the European Union, threats to infrastructure and essential services can be especially severe because so many organisations operate across borders – a single service may be critical to several nations, so a single threat can affect all of them. This also means that each nation has an obligation to its neighbours to adequately protect its critical infrastructure and services.

These are the conditions of the modern world, and protecting our infrastructure and critical services is now recognised as essential. Without electricity, water, sewage, transport and the Internet, it is essentially impossible to do business – or indeed for our modern society as a whole to function – and the EU is, after all, a major trading partnership.

The EU's Directive on security of network and information systems (NIS Directive)[5] is part of the legislated response to these threats.[6] It aims to establish a "high common level of security of network and information systems across the Union" (NIS Directive, Preamble), which will not only protect the Union's economy but also those of its trading partners, because they will benefit from the stability of the EU's infrastructure and services.

It is important to understand that the Directive is not just about cyber security or just about service continuity. It certainly requires cyber security and business continuity measures, but it is more accurately a synthesis of the two: cyber resilience. The fundamental thrust of the legislation is not simply that critical infrastructure organisations must be able to defend themselves, but that they must be able to continue functioning in the event of an incident. As part of this, there must also be a degree of

---

[5] Directive (EU) 2016/1148.

[6] Alongside legislation such as the General Data Protection Regulation (GDPR) and the ePrivacy Regulation.

communication and cooperation between EU Member States, both to share intelligence and to limit the spread of any attack.

Background

When the Directive was adopted in 2016, most EU Member States already had some regulations or laws regarding how critical infrastructure and services must be protected. These regulations and laws lacked a consistent approach, however: what one country thinks is an adequate level of cyber security may not meet their neighbour's standards, or while one country has applied conditions to a specific sector, their neighbour may not.

On the face of it, this may not appear to be a problem: a country's infrastructure should be its own concern, and it is in that country's interests to protect it, regardless of the measures its neighbours are taking or its antipathy to EU intervention. With such interconnected economies, however, and the prevalence of cross-border infrastructure and services, it is important for there to be some measure of consistency and cooperation between Member States.

The EU, as most organisations should be aware, began and remains primarily a tool for streamlining business throughout the continent. To this end, it has largely focused on standardising and formalising trade and business. The EU has two types of legal instrument that are used to regulate business:

1. **Directives**

   These set minimum standards and parameters for the EU, but leave the actual implementation down to the states themselves. When a directive is passed, the EU sets a deadline by which every Member State must have put the directive into force, whether by law, regulation or other initiative.

2. **Regulations**

   These apply across the EU with the same authority as if they were local laws. Member States may choose to pass their own laws to implement a regulation (often because the regulation requires each state to define some detail individually), but the regulation will apply regardless.

So, for any attempt to standardise practices across the Union, the EU can choose to either enforce a standard directly, or to set a minimum standard and rely on the Member States to determine more of the detail and, perhaps, to set their own standards higher. It is also worth noting that a regulation will generally set requirements intended to be applied by businesses, while directives will set conditions for states and state-run agencies.

The NIS Directive is, obviously, a directive, so each Member State will need to implement its own interpretation of the Directive's requirements. While this approach can lead to some inconsistency, every Member State is, in theory, working from a common understanding, which is a major step up from having completely divorced systems.

This differs from the treatment of the General Data Protection Regulation (GDPR), which attracted headlines at least partially because any journalist or blogger could write about it without waiting to see how the government intended to implement it.

A note on Brexit

While the UK will presumably be departing the EU in March 2019, the Directive will continue to apply after that date, much like the GDPR. This should not be a surprise: the deadline for implementing the Directive was May 2018, when the UK was still a member of the EU. Furthermore, the UK has cemented both the GDPR and the NIS Directive into UK law and regulation through the Data Protection Act 2018 and the NIS Regulations 2018, so it would be difficult (and foolish) to later renege on the commitment.

Other states have also been quick to implement the requirements of the Directive. In Germany, for instance, only minor amendments had to be made to the IT Security Act (IT-Sicherheitsgesetz) of 2015, which were completed in the

Implementation Act (Umsetzungsgesetz) of June 2017,[7] while Slovakia has passed a law "on Cybersecurity and on Amendments and Supplements to certain Acts" (o kybernetickej bezpečnosti a o zmene a doplnení niektorých zákonov).[8]

Guidance

As mentioned earlier, the UK government transposed the NIS Directive into 'The Network and Information Systems Regulations 2018 (NIS Regulations)', which was passed on 20 April 2018. This content is supported by guidance available from the National Cyber Security Centre (NCSC) and the European Union Agency for Network and Information Security (ENISA).

The UK is taking two approaches to compliance – one for each of the types of organisation described in the Directive: operators of essential services (OES) and digital service providers (DSPs). This pocket guide focuses on the requirements for OES, and its partner provides guidance for DSPs.

Key definitions

The following definitions are likely valuable to any organisation that needs to comply with the NIS Directive/Regulations. These definitions are shared between both pieces of legislation, so the risk of divergence from the original intent is diminished.

Network and information systems

a) An electronic communications network – that is, "transmission systems and, where applicable, switching or routing equipment and other resources which permit the

---

[7] Bundesamt für Sicherheit in der Infomationstechnik, "Gesetz zur Umsetzung der NIS-Richtlinie", *www.bsi.bund.de/DE/DasBSI/NIS-Richtlinie/NIS_Richtlinie_node.html*.

[8] *www.nbusr.sk/en/cyber-security/index.html*.

conveyance of signals by wire, by radio, by optical or by other electromagnetic means, including satellite networks, fixed (circuit- and packet-switched, including Internet) and mobile terrestrial networks, electricity cable systems, to the extent that they are used for the purpose of transmitting signals, networks used for radio and television broadcasting, and cable television networks, irrespective of the type of information conveyed"[9];

b) Any device or group of interconnected or related devices at least partially involved in automatic processing of digital data; or

c) Digital data stored, processed, retrieved or transmitted by one of the two elements above for their operation, use, protection and maintenance.[10]

Security of network and information systems

According to section 1(3)(g) of the NIS Regulations, this is "the ability of network and information systems to resist, at a given level of confidence, any action that compromises the availability, authenticity, integrity or confidentiality of stored or transmitted or processed data or the related services offered by, or accessible via, those network and information systems". The use of "at a given level of confidence" is particularly interesting, as it supports the notion that risk management practices are an essential element of compliance.

Incident

Under the NIS Regulations, this is "any event having an actual adverse effect on the security of network and information systems". Because it is a common term across a range of disciplines, however, it is valuable to also consider wider definitions:

---

[9] Directive 2002/21/EC, Article 2(a).

[10] Derived from NIS Directive, Article 4(1), and the NIS Regulations, section 1(2).

ISO/IEC 27000:2018 (ISO 27000, information security) provides the following definition for 'information security incident': "single or series of unwanted or unexpected information security events that have a significant probability of compromising business operations and threatening information security".

ISO 22301:2012 (ISO 22301, business continuity) provides the following definition for 'incident': "situation that might be, or could lead to, a disruption, loss, emergency or crisis".

ISO standards commonly distinguish between an event and an incident on the grounds that an 'event' is something that may or may not be an incident. ISO 27000, for instance, describes an 'information security event' as an "identified occurrence of a system, service or network state indicating a possible breach of information security policy or failure of controls, or a previously unknown situation that can be security relevant".

High common level of security

The Directive does not provide a definition for this, which leaves the actual 'level' up to negotiation between Member States. As it also aims for significantly increased cooperation across borders within the Union, the Directive will be driven by cooperation between competent authorities and computer security incident response teams (CSIRTs). This should result in a general coalescence around a set level of security in line with the priorities and objectives of businesses in the common market, and will doubtless be subject to some degree of change depending on the threats to infrastructure and the impact of the Directive on the ability to do business.

CHAPTER 1: SCOPE AND APPLICABILITY

The NIS Directive is very clear about the definitions it uses for OES. However, its approach is to provide a set of parameters and to then require each Member State to identify the precise bounds of those parameters and to "identify the operators of essential services with an establishment on their territory" (Article 5(1)).

According to the NIS Directive, an OES is an organisation that provides services that are essential for "the maintenance of critical societal and/or economic activities" (Article 5(2)), which the NIS Regulations set out in section 8(1):

> 8(1) If a person provides an essential service of a kind referred to in paragraphs 1 to 9 of Schedule 2 and that service
> —
>
> a) relies on network and information systems; and
> b) satisfies a threshold requirement described for that kind of essential service,
>
> that person is deemed to be designated as an OES for the subsector that is specified with respect to that essential service in that Schedule.

Schedule 2 of the Regulations sets out the key sectors within the UK based on the list defined in the NIS Directive, which identified the following essential sectors:

- Water (drinking water supply and distribution)
- Energy (electricity, oil and gas)
- Digital infrastructure (Internet exchange point (IXP) operators, domain name systems (DNS) and top-level domain (TLD) name registries)
- Health (healthcare providers)
- Transport (air, rail, water and road)

- Banking (credit institutions)
- Financial market infrastructures (trading venues and central counterparties)

Schedule 2 of the Regulations differs slightly from the set of sectors provided in the Directive on the basis of 'lex specialis' – there are existing special conditions in law for the banking and financial market infrastructure sectors. The UK government has determined that these sectors are already bound by equivalent provisions set by the Bank of England and the Financial Conduct Authority, and so they are exempt from the NIS Regulations. This is in line with Recital 9 of the Directive, which recognises that "Certain sectors of the economy are already regulated or may be regulated in the future by sector-specific Union legal acts that include rules related to the security of network and information systems".

It is likely there will be specific cases that do not quite fit within either the Directive's guidelines or the UK government's thresholds – the EU is, after all, a huge entity, both geographically and demographically – but the Directive requires each Member State to formally identify its OES by 9 November 2018. The UK has taken a more ambitious approach, and so all OES were required to self-identify to their competent authority by 10 August 2018. Organisations that later meet the definition of an OES are required to self-identify within three months of doing so.

In the UK, the NIS Regulations specify in section 8(3) that competent authorities are also permitted to designate some 'edge cases' OES. This can only occur if three conditions are met:

1. The OES meets the sector, subsector and essential service requirements
2. The service provided relies on network and information systems
3. An incident has the potential to significantly disrupt the provision of the essential service

The government has set itself a deadline of 10 November 2018 to identify such edge cases.

Digital service providers

While this pocket guide focuses on OES, the Directive also imposes requirements on DSPs. It is entirely possible for an organisation to provide services both as an OES and as a DSP, while for other organisations it may be less clear whether they are one or the other.

To provide some measure of clarity, the Directive specifies that DSPs are organisations that provide digital services delivered "at a distance, by electronic means and at the individual request of a recipient of services".[11] Annex III of the Directive categorises the types of services covered:

- Online search engines
- Online marketplaces
- Cloud computing services

It is also important to note that the Directive does not require Member States to identify DSPs – unlike OES, the Directive is intended to apply to DSPs across the Union without exception or variance. This is made explicit in Recital 57, which explains that "Member States should not identify digital service providers, as this Directive should apply to all digital service providers within its scope. [...] This should enable digital service providers to be treated in a uniform way across the Union".

---

[11] Directive (EU) 2015/1535, Article 1(b).

CHAPTER 2: AUTHORITIES AND BODIES

Alongside requiring Member States to set "security and notification requirements for operators of essential services and for digital service providers", the NIS Directive also specifies that they must "designate national competent authorities, single points of contact and CSIRTs with tasks related to the security of network and information systems".[12]

Each of these bodies will play an important role in how the Directive is applied in the Member States and across the EU. In the UK, the NCSC will operate as the CSIRT and the single point of contact, and as a technical authority on cyber security, all under the auspices of GCHQ.

Competent authorities

Competent authorities in the UK have been defined for each sector in the NIS Regulations. Schedule 1 of the Regulations lists the relevant government bodies that will be responsible for each sector. In the majority of cases, these are secretaries of state or ministers, who will delegate the authority to an agency under their control. The competent authority for DSPs is the Information Commissioner's Office (ICO).

Competent authorities are the organisations or agencies that oversee compliance with laws and regulations implemented on the basis of the NIS Directive. There is no specified limit on the number of competent authorities a Member State can set and several countries other than the UK have assigned them on a sectoral basis.

The primary question that each Member State needs to answer is 'What makes a competent authority competent?' Recital 30 of the Directive offers guidance:

---

[12] NIS Directive, Article 1.

In view of the differences in national governance structures and in order to safeguard already existing sectoral arrangements or Union supervisory and regulatory bodies, and to avoid duplication, Member States should be able to designate more than one national competent authority responsible for fulfilling the tasks linked to the security of the network and information systems of operators of essential services and digital service providers under this Directive.

As does Recital 61:

Competent authorities should have the necessary means to perform their duties, including powers to obtain sufficient information in order to assess the level of security of network and information systems.

Essentially, competent authorities should be able to both assess how organisations apply the principles and enforce them. As such, some authorities will doubtless be provided with additional funding or resources, and whole new agencies may be necessary for some sectors. The NIS Regulations provide specific powers for competent authorities in the UK to inspect OES and DSPs, as well as enforcement powers.

While competent authorities are regulators, the Directive makes it clear that cooperation, rather than dictatorial assertiveness, is key to making sure it is effective. As Recital 31 states:

As this Directive aims to improve the functioning of the internal market by creating trust and confidence, Member State bodies need to be able to cooperate effectively with economic actors and to be structured accordingly.

Fundamentally, the competent authorities should operate, where possible, to facilitate business rather than to repress it. 'Cooperation' is a common theme throughout the Directive, and leads into the requirements for cooperation across the EU.

CSIRTs

The Directive requires each Member State to establish a CSIRT. CSIRTs already exist in a number of countries, the most famous team almost certainly being the first – the CERT Division – which was established at Carnegie Mellon University in the US and helped to create US-CERT. In the UK, the CSIRT is the NCSC.

CSIRTs are specialist units charged with providing guidance and support in the event of a significant incident, and tracking incidents globally so that useful information and lessons can be disseminated. In relation to the NIS Directive, this means the CSIRT must be able to react appropriately to incidents that could have significant consequences for critical national infrastructure, so that their impact can be minimised. Such units will conduct research into current and evolving threats, maintain an intelligence function to identify sources of threats, keep track of vulnerabilities and suitable mitigations, and define good-practice frameworks to protect infrastructure.

A number of CSIRTs already exist across the EU, but several of these will see increases in their authority and the tools at their disposal by being established in law. As ENISA states in relation to formal, official support for the role: "an officially recognised mandate is one of the very first steps for a successful national CSIRT".[13]

The Directive states that each Member State's CSIRT should be "adequately equipped, in terms of both technical and organisational capabilities, to prevent, detect, respond to and mitigate network and information system incidents and risks" (Recital 34). Because they will act as a central resource for all OES and DSPs, the level of investment and authority they are given will be essential to the Directive's success.

All CSIRTs across the EU will be part of the CSIRTs network, which is intended to "contribute to the development of confidence and trust between the Member States and to promote swift and effective operational cooperation" (Article 12). Functionally, it will be an information-sharing arrangement with a mandate to ensure that common threats can be dealt with

---

[13] "NIS Directive and national CSIRTs", ENISA, February 2016.

through coordinated action. There are, of course, limitations on the information that can be shared, as most CSIRTs will be in some way related to national security.

Single points of contact

The single point of contact is each Member State's coordinating function for the NIS Directive. This involves coordinating the different authorities within the Member State (i.e. CSIRTs and competent authorities) as well as across the EU. The single point of contact will also receive annual reports on incidents from competent authorities and CSIRTs.

The NCSC is the UK's single point of contact, meaning that it will "act as the contact point for engagement with EU partners on [network and information systems], coordinating requests for action or information and submitting annual incident statistics".[14] If a Member State chooses to appoint only one competent authority, that body will also automatically act as the single point of contact.

Where the CSIRTs are involved in the CSIRTs network, the single point of contact will represent the Member State in the Cooperation Group described next.

Cooperation Group

The NIS Directive has established a Cooperation Group, which operates at a high level. It comprises the single points of contact from each Member State, the European Commission and ENISA. This is effectively an EU-wide governing function for protecting critical infrastructure, and has a number of important duties:

1. Providing strategic guidance for the CSIRTs network
2. Developing best-practice methods for exchanging information relating to incidents

---

[14] NCSC, "Introduction to the NIS Directive", January 2018, *www.ncsc.gov.uk/guidance/introduction-nis-directive*.

3. Evaluating national strategies on security of network and information systems
4. Coordinating information exchange with other EU institutions and offices
5. Discussing standards and specifications relevant to the NIS Directive
6. Exchanging best practice on a range of topics and practices relevant to securing critical infrastructure

Critically, the Cooperation Group will work with the Commission to produce implementing regulations that will apply across the EU, such as the Implementing Regulation of 30 January 2018, which further specified requirements for DSPs under the Directive. While these will be limited in their frequency, this is clearly an influential position critical to the ongoing security of the EU.

Powers and penalties

Within each Member State, different agencies and bodies will have differing powers to enforce the local requirements. In the UK, competent authorities can grant extensions to incident reports, which reflects the government's position that "implementing the requirements of the Directive will be realistic and will take into account the circumstances of each sector as appropriate".[15]

In addition to this, however, competent authorities will also be able to impose penalties and other regulatory actions much as the ICO can for transgressions of the GDPR.

The NIS Regulations have introduced the following range of penalties[16]:

---

[15] "Security of Network and Information Systems: Government response to public consultation".

[16] NIS Regulations 2018, s. 18(6).

- A maximum of £1 million for "any contravention [of the Regulations] which the enforcement authority determines could not cause a NIS incident".

- A maximum of £3.4 million for "a material contravention which the enforcement authority determines has caused, or could case, an incident resulting in a reduction of service provision [...] for a significant period of time".

- A maximum of £8.5 million for "a material contravention which the enforcement authority determines has caused, or could case, an incident resulting in a disruption of service provision [...] for a significant period of time".

- A maximum of £17 million for "a material contravention which the enforcement authority determines has caused, or could cause, an incident resulting in an immediate threat to life or significant adverse impact on the United Kingdom economy".

While the maximum fine is high, the government has provided assurances that OES and DSPs should not be fined under both the NIS Regulations and the GDPR for the same incident unless there is "reason for them to be penalised under different regimes for the same event because the penalties might relate to different aspects of the wrongdoing and different impacts".[17]

The level of fine is not fixed across the EU, so other Member States may set higher or lower levels as they see fit.

---

[17] "Security of Network and Information Systems: Government response to public consultation".

CHAPTER 3: COMPLYING WITH THE DIRECTIVE

As described earlier, the NIS Directive is not a piece of legislation that applies directly to organisations, so speaking of the Directive's 'requirements' is slightly misleading. The Directive does not tell organisations how to operate within the market; rather, it tells the Member States to legislate within a set of parameters – the result for the UK is the NIS Regulations.

For OES in the UK, compliance with the Regulations is through meeting requirements set by the NCSC and relevant competent authorities. The general approach that the NCSC has adopted is in line with practices internationally – which have been developed by adopting recognised best practice – including in line with the Scottish cyber resilience strategy[18] and the NIST Cybersecurity Framework (CSF),[19] so the approach is not especially novel but it is well understood.

This approach is based on recognising a small number of objectives, each of which comprises a number of principles. By focusing on objectives and principles, organisations can develop their own structured approach to compliance, and can apply the objectives and principles in line with their needs and business environment. In the NCSC's own words, "The NIS cyber security principles define a set of top-level outcomes that,

---

[18] Scottish Government, "A Cyber Resilience Strategy for Scotland: Public sector action plan 2017-2018", 2017, *https://beta.gov.scot/publications/cyber-resilience-strategy-scotland-public-sector-action-plan-2017-18/*.

[19] National Institutes of Standards and Technology, "Framework for Improving Critical Infrastructure Cybersecurity", 2014, *www.nist.gov/cyberframework*.

collectively, describes good cyber security for operators of essential services".[20]

Cyber security objectives

The NCSC has set four top-level objectives:

1. Managing security risk
2. Protecting against cyber attack
3. Detecting cyber security events
4. Minimising the impact of cyber security incidents

People who have looked over other approaches to cyber security may recognise similarities with other frameworks, although those tend to use simpler terms to describe the objectives, such as 'identify', 'protect', 'detect', 'respond' and 'recover'. While the NCSC approach is wordier, it also captures some of the subtlety and detail of the approach that might be lost if you only consider the frameworks from a degree of detachment. For instance, the first objective makes it clearer that risk management is an integral part of effective cyber security and is more than simply 'identifying' threats.

The objectives are primarily a device for arranging the 14 principles. In providing objectives, however, organisations can align them with their existing objectives and integrate them with any existing procedures, such as board oversight, project management, and so on.

Principles

The principles are the meat of the UK government's approach to complying with the NIS Directive. Each principle is aligned with a specific objective, and, as the NCSC states, "Each principle describes mandatory security outcomes to be achieved".[21] In this

---

[20] NCSC, "Introduction to the NIS Directive", January 2018, *www.ncsc.gov.uk/guidance/introduction-nis-directive*.

[21] NCSC, "NIS Directive: Top-level objectives", January 2018, *www.ncsc.gov.uk/guidance/nis-directive-top-level-objectives*.

sense, the principles effectively set control objectives: what do the measures need to achieve to manage threats to the organisation? Because the principles focus on outcomes rather than specific practices, it is up to the organisation to decide how it actually goes about achieving them.

The following table provides some clarity on the principles.

Table 1: Objectives and Principles

A. Managing security risk	Objective: Appropriate organisational structures, policies and processes in place to understand, assess and systematically manage security risks to the network and information systems supporting essential services.
A.1 Governance	The organisation takes a proactive approach to cyber security and, by extension, protection of national infrastructure and essential services, led from and overseen by the top of the organisation. The organisation clearly assigns responsibilities and accountability for protecting the organisation's services, and has appropriate processes in place to make decisions related to protecting network and information systems.
A.2 Risk management	The organisation takes a risk-based approach to identifying threats and managing the organisation's exposure, and is able to follow up the risk management process to confirm its effectiveness. Risk management will be discussed

	in the next chapter as part of our recommended approach to complying with the NIS Directive.
A.3 Asset management	This relates to the need to ensure that assets are appropriately understood so that they can be correctly supplied and managed, and so that dependencies are appreciated and can be taken into account in the event of an incident. The principle makes it clear that this includes "data, people and systems, as well as any supporting infrastructure".
A.4 Supply chain	While an organisation may outsource some risk or investment by using third parties to supply elements of their services (or supporting utilities/goods/services), the organisation itself remains responsible for delivering its services. Consumers and the broader public need to be confident that these services will continue to be supplied, regardless of whether a third party is involved. In essence, this is about securing risks to the organisation's supply chain – are the organisation's suppliers reliable? Is the organisation able to find alternative suppliers in an emergency?
B. Protecting against cyber attack	**Objective: Proportionate security measures in place to**

	protect essential services and systems from cyber attack.
B.1 Service protection policies and processes	The organisation's policies and processes describe how the organisation protects itself from incidents and, by extension, its services from disruption. There are two crucial elements to this: development and implementation. This principle ensures that the organisation can develop effective cyber security policies and procedures, and apply them consistently and effectively.
B.2 Identity and access control	The organisation should ensure that identity is verified before giving any user access to any network or information system, and this should be a more rigorous process where devices provide access to critical systems or information. Access to specific systems should be linked to that identity so that permissions can be granted (or restricted) in accordance with need and to log what each person does while granted access to networks and information systems. Depending on need and the specific systems, this could mean prohibiting the use of shared or guest accounts.
B.3 Data security	Access to information is controlled at all stages, including in transit and storage, and when hardware is disposed of. This is a broad principle that accounts for many of the

	functions of traditional information security, particularly the preservation of the confidentiality, integrity and availability of information assets. In order to adequately protect data, the organisation must ensure that it understands the data and its needs.
B.4 System security	The systems by which information is transmitted, stored, accessed or manipulated must be protected. This may include software operating on network and information systems, as well as the physical elements of the networks and information systems themselves. This should span the whole lifecycle of the system: system design, use of secure configurations, secure management, and managing vulnerabilities as and when they arise.
B.5 Resilient networks and systems	Resilience refers to an organisation's combined ability to prepare for, meet and respond to incidents. This means that an organisation minimises the immediate and ongoing impact of an incident, as well as reducing the recovery time. This principle notes that this should be taken into account in "the design, implementation, operation and management of systems that support the delivery of essential services". As such, this will require a thorough set of formal processes to identify resilience

	requirements for networks and systems that can be incorporated during the design phase.
B.6 Staff awareness and training	Developing and promoting a culture of cyber security is essential. Staff should be given appropriate information and training so that they can support the security of network and information systems. Staff need to know how to operate security measures on a day-to-day basis, how to report incidents and what their roles are during recovery. The organisation should also ensure that all employees are suitably competent for their roles to support any requirements for cyber security that they might need to work with.
C. Detecting cyber security events	**Objective: Capabilities to ensure security defences remain effective and to detect cyber security events affecting, or with the potential to affect, essential services.**
C.1 Security monitoring	Monitoring the security of network and information systems requires processes and technologies to identify whether security systems and processes are functioning correctly. It is important to understand that this principle requires the organisation to detect both potential security problems (such as a previously unidentified vulnerability) and failures in protective security

	measures. This should ensure that security is a continuous process rather than something that is applied once and forgotten. Sources of data should be reliable and provide information about events as soon as possible.
C.2 Anomaly detection	Systems involved in providing essential services are proactively monitored for evidence of an incident. The key will be identifying what is 'normal' and generating alerts when a system deviates from this. In particular, the principle specifies that the organisation must implement measures to detect anomalies "even when the activity evades standard signature based security prevent/detect solutions".
D. Minimising the impact of cyber security incidents	**Objective: Capabilities to minimise the impacts of a cyber security incident on the delivery of essential services including the restoration of those services where necessary.**
D.1 Response and recovery planning	The organisation must be prepared for incidents and have plans to ensure continuity of services in the event of disruption. These will include plans for incident response, impact mitigation and recovery, and should be supported by making sure the organisation has the resources and capacity to enact them. They should be

	developed based on the organisation's risk management approach, and should be tested regularly to confirm they are adequate.
D.2 Improvements	The organisation must be able to learn from incidents (through root-cause analysis, for instance) and make amendments and improvements to its security and resilience measures where necessary. A process should be in place to regularly review these measures and implement any identifiable improvements.

Each principle is supported by a body of guidance, including references to existing best-practice standards and frameworks.[22] These provide information that an organisation can adopt and adapt to help them implement the requirements of each of the principles. The guidance also avoids specifying technologies, focusing instead on describing processes and outcomes, and allowing the organisation to select technologies and practices in line with its business needs and environment.

Cyber Assessment Framework

First – and perhaps foremost – the Cyber Assessment Framework (CAF) is not a framework for complying with the Directive: it is a framework for competent authorities to determine whether an organisation has applied appropriate measures to protect the security of network and information systems. As the NCSC states, it is not "a checklist to be used in

---

[22] NCSC, "NIS Directive: Table view of principles and related guidance", January 2018, *www.ncsc.gov.uk/guidance/table-view-principles-and-related-guidance*.

an inflexible assessment process".[23] Having said that, it does provide an excellent model for validating your organisation's cyber security measures.

The CAF breaks each principle down into outcomes, which are further broken down into 'indicators of good practice' (IGPs). These are simple descriptions of the 'symptoms' an assessor should expect to see if the organisation has correctly applied the principle. As mentioned earlier, the principles are not concerned with how you go about achieving them, only that the outcomes are adequate to protect the organisation and the services it provides.

The outcomes provide implicit guidance as to what is expected by identifying the key characteristics of each principle. For instance, while Principle A1 is 'governance' and the guidance describes what governance is in relation to the NIS Directive and where to find further information about implementing governance, the outcomes subdivide this into three practices:

1. Board direction
2. Roles and responsibilities
3. Decision-making

Outcomes are written generically to ensure they can be applied widely. For example:

> You contextualise alerts with knowledge of the threat and your systems, to identify those security incidents that require some form of response.

This allows them to be applied to any organisation, regardless of the technologies used, the organisational structure, and so on. Each outcome is then broken down into a set of IGPs that are more detailed while remaining widely applicable. For instance:

> You have selected threat intelligence feeds using risk-based and threat-informed decisions based on your business needs

---

[23] NCSC, "NIS Directive: Top-level objectives", January 2018, *www.ncsc.gov.uk/guidance/nis-directive-top-level-objectives*.

and sector (e.g. vendor reporting and patching, strong antivirus providers, sector and community-based infoshare).

You are able to apply new signatures and [indicators of compromise] within a reasonable (risk-based) time of receiving them.

As you can see, these IGPs provide a level of granularity that can help the organisation to understand what is expected of it and what level of detail it should go to in applying the principles. Having a generic process for examining threats will not suffice; for example, the organisation must ensure that it gathers the right information and seeks guidance and support from appropriate sources. Whatever process the organisation applies must demonstrate a minimum set of IGPs in order to achieve the desired outcomes.

Competent authorities are responsible for determining how the CAF applies to their sector. The authorities are explicitly permitted to pick and choose from the CAF to create assessment profiles appropriate to the organisations that they regulate. It is, therefore, essential that you seek clarity from your competent authority on what exactly it will want to assess. The NCSC states that competent authorities might define sector-specific requirements as follows:

i. Sector-specific CAF profiles
ii. Sector-specific Interpretations of Contributing Outcomes/IGPs
iii. Sector-specific Additional Contributing Outcomes/IGPs

A 'profile' is the set of outcomes and IGPs against which the competent authority will assess OES. As noted above, this may not comprise the full set of outcomes and IGPs provided by the CAF.

The second power permits competent authorities to modify or reinterpret the outcomes and IGPs in accordance with the needs of the sector. For instance, the way an organisation involved in the supply of water applies each principle may differ wildly from the way it is applied by an organisation involved in air freight. Equally, a competent authority may seek more specific outcomes and IGPs, perhaps in relation to sector-specific technologies or processes.

The last power is worthy of special attention as it permits competent authorities to assess additional outcomes or IGPs, which you may not be able to find by simply looking up the NCSC guidance. The guidance states that "There may be circumstances in which sector-specific cyber security requirements cannot be adequately covered by an interpretation of a generic contributing outcome or IGP. In these cases, an additional sector-specific contributing outcome or IGP may need to be defined".[24] In order to ensure you meet the NIS Regulations' requirements, you will need to confirm the specific set of outcomes and IGPs against which you will be assessed by your competent authority.

Each outcome can be achieved to varying levels, and the competent authority will determine the level necessary for its sector. In some instances, an organisation may only need to 'partially achieve' an outcome in accordance with the requirements for the sector.

Under the NIS Regulations, competent authorities are not required to assess compliance on a regular basis, but they do have two specific powers that are likely to relate to the CAF. The first of these is that competent authorities can serve OES with an information notice:

> (2) A designated competent authority may serve an information notice upon an OES requiring that person to provide it with information that it reasonably requires to assess —

---

[24] NCSC, "Introduction to the Cyber Assessment Framework", April 2018, *www.ncsc.gov.uk/guidance/introduction-cyber-assessment-framework*.

(a) the security of the OES's network and information systems; and

(b) the implementation of the operator's security policies, including any about inspections conducted under regulation 16 and any underlying evidence in relation to such an inspection.[25]

The second is the right of inspection referred to in (b), which puts additional requirements on OES and DSPs. As the NIS Regulations state:

(3) For the purposes of carrying out the inspection [...] the OES or [relevant DSP] (as the case may be) must—

(a) pay the reasonable costs of the inspection;

(b) co-operate with the person who is conducting the inspection ("the inspector");

(c) provide the inspector with reasonable access to their premises;

(d) allow the inspector to inspect, copy or remove such documents and information, including information that is held electronically, as the inspector considers to be relevant to the inspection; and

(e) allow the inspector access to any person from whom the inspector seeks relevant information for the purposes of the inspection.[26]

Obviously, it is sensible for any organisation to minimise friction at all points, so organisations should ensure that they can provide evidence of all outcomes and IGPs in their CAF profile, and that this evidence is readily available. In the majority of cases, this will mean making sure that each IGP is habitual

---

[25] NIS Regulations 2018, s. 15(2).

[26] NIS Regulations 2018, s. 16(3).

within the organisation: the practices should be part of business as usual.

Notifications

As part of day-to-day compliance with the NIS Regulations, OES must be prepared to notify authorities in the event of an incident. The Regulations state that this should be done "without undue delay and in any event not later than 72 hours after the [OES] is aware that a NIS incident has occurred".[27] The government has also stated that voluntary reporting (for incidents that pose little or no risk to essential services) can be made to either the competent authority or the CSIRT (the NCSC).[28]

The Directive also makes an important distinction: the OES is only required to notify if there is a "significant impact". Each Member State will determine its own definition for "significant impact", and in the UK this has been left to the individual competent authorities. The government has defined three parameters for determining what a 'significant impact' is:

1. The number of users affected by the disruption of the essential service.
2. The duration of the incident.
3. The geographical area affected by the incident.[29]

All OES should be able to request information about the sector's definition of 'significant' from their competent authority. It is worth noting that the NCSC (in its role as CSIRT) can also determine whether an incident is significant on the basis of the information provided in an incident notification.[30]

---

[27] NIS Regulations 2018, s. 11(3)(b)(i).

[28] "Security of Network and Information Systems: Government response to public consultation".

[29] NIS Regulations 2018, s. 11(2).

[30] NIS Regulations 2018, s. 11(6).

In many cases, OES will not be reasonably able to immediately determine whether an incident is significant, and it would be sensible to report any incident that could develop into something significant – not least so that the NCSC can make that determination on the basis of expertise.

Following notification, the competent authority will determine whether a follow-up investigation is necessary. Accommodations for these investigations should not be included in the organisation's incident response – as the government noted in its response to the consultation, it "will be a standalone process and will not form any part of the incident response".

Where an organisation might decide that it needs support for the incident response, it can notify the NCSC in much the same way as the competent authority.

CHAPTER 4: IMPLEMENTING CYBER RESILIENCE

As mentioned in the introduction, the full set of practices that support the 14 principles and 4 objectives set out by the NCSC is often described as 'cyber resilience'. It is a blend of cyber security, incident response and business continuity. The principle behind cyber resilience is that an organisation can do a great deal to prevent incidents or mitigate their impact, but incidents remain inevitable. An effective cyber resilience framework protects an organisation from the majority of attacks and incidents, while also maximising its durability when an incident does occur.

As the technology to commit cyber crime becomes more intelligent and the number of vulnerabilities that any organisation might be subject to increases, the threat of a cyber attack increases. This assumption is supported by statistics: according to a 2018 UK government survey,[31] 43% of all UK businesses had suffered at least one breach or cyber attack in the previous 12 months, which was higher among medium-sized (64%) and large organisations (72%) – and this is despite a significant increase in investment in cyber security.

For organisations that do suffer an incident, such as a cyber attack, it is critical that they have processes in place to respond, reduce its impact and quickly recover to business as usual. It is sensible to look not just at your legal requirements (those of the NIS Directive, in this case), but to look for a solution that is best able to protect the organisation. For this reason, we favour a more complete approach to cyber resilience – one that incorporates a full set of continuity processes to minimise disruption and associated costs. This requires a comprehensive

---

[31] Department for Digital, Culture, Media & Sport, "Cyber Security Breaches Survey 2018", April 2018, *www.gov.uk/government/statistics/cyber-security-breaches-survey-2018*.

framework that considers people, processes and technology – and people are arguably the most important part of that because they are, after all, critical to ensuring that processes and technologies are applied correctly and consistently.

Just as the principles adopted by the NCSC assert, the project must be led from the top of the organisation, and must be capable of continually adapting to new threats and changing environments. These are characteristics of any successful, ongoing business project, and it is true that cyber resilience should be treated in much the same way.

An organisation could develop a cyber resilience capability by simply going through the guidance and references provided by the NCSC, but this is likely to result in an inconsistent and disorganised set of processes without a larger appreciation for how they fit into the organisation. A successful project must take a more considered, holistic approach.

ISO standards – especially ISO/IEC 27001:2013 (information security) and ISO 22301:2012 (business continuity) – provide specifications for management systems that can be integrated to provide an effective framework for cyber resilience, incorporating further guidance from standards such as ISO 27002 and ISO 27035.

However, helpful as these standards may be, they are not designed for compliance with the NIS Directive, NIS Regulations or any other piece of legislation. Rather, they are intended to provide guidance on good practice to protect information and information systems (the ISO 27000 family), and help organisations survive and quickly recover from incidents (ISO 22301). As such, any organisation using these standards to any degree still needs to ensure that it has taken all steps necessary to achieve, maintain and prove compliance.

ISO 27001 and ISO 27002

ISO 27001 is the international standard for information security management, and provides a structured approach to protecting an organisation's information assets. Meanwhile, ISO 27002 –

the 'code of practice' – provides comprehensive implementation guidance that builds on ISO 27001.

Like other ISO management system standards, ISO 27001 recognises that there are a number of core functions that any management system must rely upon and builds onto them. This makes information security part of the way the organisation operates, rather than simply being a side concern. This also takes into account the organisation's business environment and obligations, ensuring that the information security management system (ISMS) is relevant to the organisation.

This begins with top management commitment, in line with NCSC's principle A1 (governance). The organisation must both direct and support the ISMS from the very top, which might be the board or senior management, and includes taking accountability for the success of the project. This ensures that the ISMS can be operated in line with the organisation's wider business objectives, while also providing evidence that information security is a topic to be taken very seriously.

In line with Recital 44 of the Directive, "A culture of risk management, involving risk assessment and the implementation of security measures appropriate to the risks faced, should be promoted and developed through appropriate regulatory requirements and voluntary industry practices", ISO 27001 advocates taking a risk management approach to information security (see NCSC principle A2). In other words, the organisation should decide how to mitigate its risk on the basis of an informed assessment of the risks it actually faces.

Once again, this exists within a larger framework that takes the organisation's business environment into account. ISO 27001's risk management process is kept deliberately open to allow the organisation to use whatever methodology is already familiar or appropriate to the business. Rather than prescribing a method in detail, it simply sets out a more general process that can be adopted by most risk management methodologies.

Clause 6.1 of ISO 27001 requires the organisation's risk assessment process to:

- Define both risk acceptance criteria and criteria for conducting a risk assessment;
- Produce "consistent, valid and comparable results";
- Identify risks associated with the loss of confidentiality, integrity and availability of information assets;
- Analyse the risks to identify the likelihood of it occurring and the potential impact if it does occur; and
- Evaluate the risks against the organisation's risk acceptance criteria to decide upon appropriate responses.

While this can become a complex process that requires specific expertise, the NCSC principles provide further guidance on the matter and refer to a number of risk management frameworks, including ISO 27005, which is aligned with ISO 27001.

The output of risk assessment will be a risk treatment plan that describes how the organisation will treat the risks it has identified. For the most part, this will involve applying controls. Such controls can fulfil a range of functions, but they generally fall into one of three categories:

1. **Preventive**
   Preventive controls are intended to prevent risks from occurring or to reduce their likelihood. For instance, a rigorous patching programme reduces the amount of time that applications are vulnerable to exploitation, which in turn reduces the likelihood that an attacker will be able to take advantage of them.

2. **Detective**
   Detective controls identify events and incidents, allowing the organisation to take steps to prevent an incident from occurring, gather forensic evidence for later action or react to reduce the impact of an incident. For instance, an intrusion detection system (IDS) identifies anomalous activity that could be an intrusion into the organisation's networks. This activity may not be an actual intrusion, but it could be symptomatic of a vulnerability that the organisation can then act to resolve.

3. **Reactive**
   Reactive controls come into play when an event or

incident occurs and seek to reduce their impact. For instance, a process that isolates a network segment can prevent an attacker from exfiltrating data, progressing further into the system or identifying further weaknesses to exploit.

It is, of course, possible for a control to fulfil several functions – a CCTV camera might discourage a criminal from breaking into an office (preventive), identify when a break-in occurs (detective) and help identify the intruder (reactive). Meanwhile, a firewall is primarily preventive in that it tries to keep intruders out, but can also function as a detective control by notifying the user of suspicious activity.

As said earlier, it is important to understand that the organisation should select controls on the basis of the actual risks it faces, and should balance the cost of treating a risk against the impact of the risk. As part of this, the organisation should be sure that it understands the 'hidden' costs of an incident, including reputational damage, legal harm, and regulatory action including fines. Annex A of ISO 27001 provides a reference set of controls that are generally applicable and supported by guidance in ISO 27002, but organisations are free to draw their controls from any source or design their own.

Many controls will also directly contribute towards meeting the requirements of the NCSC's principles – for instance, controls concerning asset management align with principle A3, a wide range of controls can contribute to data security (principle B3), and so on. Risks to each of the principles (i.e. the risk that the principle will not be achieved) should also be taken into account in order to protect the organisation's ability to protect itself from incidents that could disrupt its services.

There is a great deal more that could be said on the topic of risk management. For more information, read *Information Security Risk Management for ISO27001/ISO27002*.[32]

The controls to directly manage risks are supported by a range of management procedures that tie information security into 'ordinary' business processes. These include communication, competence and staff awareness (see NCSC principle B6), which ensure that the ISMS is well understood and that the organisation has the skills and knowledge to implement and maintain it.

The ISMS must also be assessed to make sure it is functioning correctly and in line with the documented processes. This is achieved through a combination of ongoing, regular measurements and internal audits. The results of these assessments are then reviewed by management so that any discrepancies or anomalies can be resolved. Just as management must initiate and support the ISMS, it is also responsible for ensuring its continuing efficacy. This set of processes allows the organisation to continually improve the ISMS, which ensures it remains effective over time and in the face of changing technologies and environments.

Another key component of an ISO 27001-conforming ISMS, and possibly part of this set of processes, is penetration testing – systematic and controlled probing for vulnerabilities in your applications and networks. Regular penetration testing is the most effective way of identifying exploitable vulnerabilities in your infrastructure, allowing appropriate mitigation to be applied. It would also be good practice to test any new services or networks before making them available. Vulnerabilities are discovered and exploited all the time by opportunistic criminal hackers who use automated scans to identify targets. Closing these security gaps and fixing vulnerabilities as soon as they

---

[32] Alan Calder and Steve Watkins, 2010, *www.itgovernance.co.uk/shop/product/information-security-risk-management-for-iso27001iso27002*.

become known are essential steps to keeping your networks and information systems safe and secure.

ISO 22301

Many of the same processes used in information security management apply to a business continuity management system (BCMS) aligned to ISO 22301 – in particular, the more general management processes, such as ensuring management oversight and review, communication, awareness, competence and documentation management. This means that they can be applied simultaneously to integrate both management systems. For instance, the same process used to make staff aware of the organisation's need for information security can also be used to stress the importance of continuity – even within the same breath, if need be. Because these processes are shared, the organisation can save time and money by integrating these management systems.

A BCMS that conforms to ISO 22301 provides a well-defined incident response structure, ensuring that when an incident occurs, responses are escalated in a timely manner and the right people take the right actions to respond effectively. The key processes involved in a BCMS are business impact analysis (BIA), risk assessment and the business continuity plan (BCP), and align with NCSC principle D1.

BIA is the process of identifying the impact on the organisation if a given business function is disrupted. It also takes into account how that impact changes over time. After all, some incidents will have a very small or negligible impact unless they persist, while other incidents have an immediate impact that does not change over time.

This information then becomes the basis for prioritising each business process for recovery in the event of a disruptive incident. For OES, additional weight should be given to services and processes that support service delivery.

ISO 22301's approach to risk assessment focuses on risks to "the organization's prioritized activities and the processes, systems, information, people, assets, outsource partners and other resources that support them".[33] Treatment of these risks should be in line with both the organisation's continuity objectives and its risk appetite. These objectives should, of course, include the objectives set by the NCSC.

By combining the assessed threat that each risk poses to the organisation's critical services, the organisation is able to prioritise its responses. These priorities inform the BCP(s).

The BCP is critical to the BCMS: it describes how the organisation will respond to disruptions, in both general and specific terms. For instance, it should include contact details for authorities and key suppliers, and sources of support that can be called on during disruptions, while also setting out the detailed steps involved in responding to and recovering from incidents that affect the organisation's critical services.

The BCP relies on being tested regularly. Without testing, there is little way of knowing whether the plan is effective, or of improving the plan to better protect the organisation's ability to respond to and recover from disruptive incidents.

ISO 27035

ISO 27035 outlines concepts, phases and overall guidelines for information security incident management, and can be easily implemented by organisations also aiming to meet ISO 27001's requirements, as many of the two standards' processes line up. As previously explained, ISO 27035's structured approach to incident response consists of five phases:

1. Plan and prepare
2. Detection and reporting
3. Assessment and decision
4. Responses
5. Lessons learnt

---

[33] ISO 22301:2012, Clause 8.2.3 a).

The first phase, detailed in Clause 5.2 of the Standard, focuses on the more general management processes, such as ensuring management oversight and review, communication, awareness, competence and documentation management.

The second phase becomes more specific for information security incident management, which is dedicated to internally reporting potential incidents as soon as possible after any unusual activity has been detected.

The third phase, assessment and decision, looks into assessing the situation and deciding whether the event classifies as an 'information security incident'. If so, the incident has to be contained, information has to be collected to pinpoint what exactly happened, and a log has to be kept, which can be analysed at a later stage.

In the fourth phase, responses, any agreed incident management activities have to be carried out after tasks and responsibilities have been assigned. Such activities could include reviewing any reports made and logs kept, reassessing the damage and notifying the relevant people or bodies. This point is particularly relevant for the Directive's purpose, as any incident of substantial impact has to be reported.

Finally, after all urgent action has been taken, the whole situation and process can be reviewed, including any existing management systems, plans or procedures, and notes can be taken on how the incident could have been mitigated or even prevented. The most important part of "lessons learnt" is ensuring that potential improvements are actually implemented.

Combining standards

With an ISO 27001-aligned ISMS in place and integrated with an ISO 22301-aligned BCMS, taking note of incident response procedures as guided by ISO 27035, the organisation has a systematic approach to cyber resilience and compliance with relevant laws and regulations, including the NIS Directive.

Because these management systems operate on a process of continual improvement, they can adapt to changes in the legal environment and evolving threats. This is critical: an organisation that cannot continue to defend itself from cyber attack and other incidents will inevitably suffer, and regulators will see this and act accordingly. Cyber resilience is an ongoing concern that should adapt and grow as an organisation does, not a project to complete once and leave to stagnate.

APPENDIX: OES DEFINITIONS AND THRESHOLDS

Sector	Subsector	Essential service	Identification thresholds
Drinking water supply and distribution	N/A	The supply of potable water to households.	Operators with sites serving 200,000 or more people.
Energy	Electricity	The function of supply (the sale or resale of electricity) to consumers.	In England, Scotland and Wales: Electricity suppliers (including aggregators where they act as suppliers) that meet the following two criteria (both must apply): • Use of smart metering infrastructure. • Supply > 250,000 consumers. Operators of electricity generators[34] with a generating capacity ≥ 2 gigawatts (GW), including: • Standalone transmission connected generation; and • Multiple generating units with a cumulative capaclty ≥ 2GW controlled by an individual/

---

[34] Excluding nuclear electricity generation. The government does not consider the civil nuclear sector to be in scope of the NIS Directive.

Sector	Subsector	Essential service	Identification thresholds
			common control network.
			In Northern Ireland: Licensed suppliers that supply to > 8,000 customers.
			And any generator with a generating capacity ≥ 350MW.
		Electricity (SEM operator).	The holder of a SEM operator licence under Article 8(1)(d) of the Electricity (NI) Order 1992.
		Electricity (transmission).	In England, Scotland and Wales: Network operators with the potential to disrupt supply to > 250,000 consumers.
			International interconnectors and DC converter station with a capacity ≥ 1GW.
			In Northern Ireland: Holders of a transmission licence under Article 8(1)(b) of the Electricity (NI) Order 1992.
		Electricity (distribution).	In England, Scotland and Wales: Network operators with the potential to disrupt supply to > 250,000 consumers.
			In Northern Ireland: Holders of a distribution licence under Article 8(1)(bb) of the Electricity (NI) Order 1992.

Sector	Subsector	Essential service	Identification thresholds
	Oil	Oil transmission (upstream).	Operators with throughput of more than 20 million barrels of oil equivalent (BOE) of oil per year.
		Oil transmission (downstream). The distribution of petroleum-based fuels to other storage sites throughout the UK by road, pipeline, rail or ship.	In England, Scotland and Wales: Operators that provide or handle 500,000 tonnes of fuel per year. In Northern Ireland: Operators that provide or handle 50,000 tonnes of fuel per year.
		Oil production, refining and treatment and storage (upstream).	Operators with throughput of 20 million BOE of oil per year.
		Oil production, refining and treatment and storage (downstream). – The import of any of crude oil, intermediates, components and finished fuels. – The storage of any of crude oil, intermediates, components and finished fuels. – The production of intermediates, components and finished fuels through a range of refining or blending processes. – The distribution of petroleum-based fuels to	In England, Scotland and Wales: Operators that provide or handle 500,000 tonnes of fuel/per year. In Northern Ireland: Operators that have a storage capacity > 50,000 tonnes of fuel.

Sector	Subsector	Essential service	Identification thresholds
		other storage sites throughout the UK by road, pipeline, rail or ship. – The delivery of petroleum-based fuels to retail sites, airports or end users.	
	Gas	The function of supply (the sale or resale of gas) to consumers.	In England, Scotland and Wales: Gas suppliers (including aggregators where they act as suppliers) that meet the following two criteria (both must apply): • Use of smart metering infrastructure. • Supply > 250,000 consumers. In Northern Ireland: Licensed suppliers that supply to > 2,000 customers.
		Gas (transmission) (downstream).	In England, Scotland and Wales: Network operators with the potential to disrupt supply to > 250,000 consumers. Operators of gas interconnectors with technical capacity > 20mcm/d. In Northern Ireland: Holders of a licence under Article 8(1)(a) of the Gas (NI) Order 1996.
		Gas (distribution).	In England, Scotland and Wales:

Sector	Subsector	Essential service	Identification thresholds
			Network operators with the potential to disrupt supply to > 250,000 consumers. In Northern Ireland: Holders of a licence under Article 8(1)(a) of the Gas (NI) Order 1996.
		Gas storage facilities supplying/storing gas for the national transmission network.	In England, Scotland and Wales: Operators with the potential to input > 20mcm/d to the national transmission network. In Northern Ireland: Holders of a licence under Article 8(1)(b) of the Gas (NI) Order 1996.
		LNG system operators supplying/storing gas for the national transmission network.	In England, Scotland and Wales: Operators with the potential to input > 20mcm/d to the national transmission network. In Northern Ireland: Holders of a licence under Article 8(1)(d) of the Gas (NI) Order 1996.
		Gas (transmission) (upstream).	Operators with throughput of more than 20 million BOE of gas per year.
		Gas (production, refining and treatment)	Operators with throughput of more than 20 million BOE of gas per year.
Digital infrastructure	N/A	Top-level domain (TLD) name registries.	Operators that service an average of 2 billion queries or more in 24 hours for

Sector	Subsector	Essential service	Identification thresholds
			domains registered within ICANN. Note: this threshold is an annual average and shall be based on the best available data from the preceding 12 months. Note: the threshold excludes growth of traffic load due to malicious activity such as distributed denial-of-service attacks.
		Domain name services (DNS) service providers.	Operators that provide DNS resolution and which service an average of 2 million queries or more in 24 hours. Operators that provide authoritative hosting of domain names, offered for use by publicly accessible services, servicing $\geq$ 250,000 different domain names. Note: this threshold is an annual average and shall be based on the best available data from the preceding 12 months.
		IXP operators.	Operators that have $\geq$ 50% annual market share among UK IXP operators in terms of interconnected autonomous systems, or that offer interconnectivity to $\geq$ 50% of global Internet routes.

Sector	Subsector	Essential service	Identification thresholds
			Note: 'interconnected autonomous system' is defined in NIS Directive Article 4 (13). Note: 'global Internet route' means: the total number of active entries within the Global Internet Routing Table, averaged per calendar year.
Health sector	Healthcare settings	Healthcare services.	In England: Providers of non-primary NHS healthcare commissioned under the National Health Service Act 2006 as amended in England (but not including any individual doctors providing such healthcare). In Wales: Local health boards and NHS trusts (defined by the National Health Service (Wales) Act 2006). In Scotland: The 14 territorial health boards; the following four special NHS boards: NHS National Waiting Times Centre, NHS24, Scottish Ambulance Service and The State Hospitals Board for Scotland; and Common Services Scotland (known as NHS National Services Scotland).

Sector	Subsector	Essential service	Identification thresholds
			In Northern Ireland: Health and social care trusts (defined by Health and Social Care (Reform) Act (Northern Ireland) 2009).
Transport	Air transport	Owner or operator of an aerodrome (as defined in the Civil Aviation Act 1982).	Owner or operator of any aerodrome (i.e. airport) with annual terminal passenger numbers greater than 10 million.
		Provider of air traffic services (as defined in the Transport Act 2000).	Any entity that is licensed to provide UK en route air traffic services. Air traffic service providers at airports with annual terminal passenger numbers greater than 10 million.
		Air carriers (as defined in paragraph 4 of Article 3 of Regulation (EC) No 300/2008).	Air carriers with more than 30% of the annual terminal passengers at any individual UK airport that is in scope of the Directive and more than 10 million total annual terminal passengers across all UK airports.
	Maritime transport	Harbour authorities (as defined in the Merchant Shipping Act 1995). Operators of vessel traffic services (as defined in the Merchant Shipping (Vessel Traffic	Harbour authorities or operators at ports with annual passenger numbers > 10 million. Or at ports that account for: • 15% of UK total Roll on-Roll off (Ro-Ro) traffic; • 15% of UK total Lift on-Lift off (Lo-Lo) traffic;

Sector	Subsector	Essential service	Identification thresholds
		Monitoring and Reporting Requirements) Regulations 2004 SI 2004/2110).	• 10% of UK total liquid bulk; or • 20% of UK biomass fuel.
		Operators of a port facility (as defined in the Port Security Regulations 2009 – SI 2009/2048).	Operators of port facilities at ports that meet the above thresholds and that handle the type of freight specified in those thresholds.
		Passenger and freight water transport companies (as defined for maritime transport in Annex I to Regulation (EC) No 725/2004).	Operators that handle more than 30% of the freight at any individual UK port that is in scope and more than 5 million tonnes of total annual freight at UK ports. Operators that have more than 30% of the annual passenger numbers at any individual UK port that is in scope and more than 2 million total annual passengers at UK ports.
	Rail transport	Operators of any railway asset (as defined in section 6 of the Railways Act 1993) on the mainline railway network. This will include operators of trains, networks, stations and light maintenance depots, where operating those assets on the mainline railway network.	Any operator of a railway asset on the mainline railway network (as defined).

Sector	Subsector	Essential service	Identification thresholds
		Railway undertaking as defined in the Northern Ireland Transport Act 1967. The mainline railway network will be defined to include all railways in GB but will exclude: i. International rail; ii. Metros, trams and light rail systems; iii. Heritage, museum or tourist railways whether or not they are operating solely on their own network; and iv. Networks that are privately owned and exist solely for use by the infrastructure owner for its own freight operations or other activities not involving passenger or freight services for third parties.	
		Operators of railway assets (as defined in section 6 of the Railways Act 1993) for metros, trams and light rail	Operators with annual passenger journeys greater than 50 million.

Sector	Subsector	Essential service	Identification thresholds
		(including underground) systems.	
		Operators of international rail services.	Any operator of a Channel Tunnel train (as defined in the Channel Tunnel Security Order 1994). Any operator of international rail services in Northern Ireland, as defined in the Northern Ireland Transport Act 1967.
		International rail infrastructure managers.	Any infrastructure manager of the Channel Fixed Link, i.e. the Concessionaires (as defined in the Channel Tunnel Act 1987). Any infrastructure manager of international rail services in Northern Ireland, as defined in the Northern Ireland Transport Act 1967.
	Road transport	Road authorities as defined in point (12) of Article 2 of the Commission Delegated Regulation (EU) 2015/962.	A road authority responsible for roads in the UK that annually in total have vehicles travelling > 50 billion miles on them.
		Operators of intelligent transport systems as defined in point (1) of Article 4 of Directive 2010/40/EU of the European Parliament and of the Council.	A road authority that provides an intelligent transport systems service that covers roads in the UK that annually in total have vehicles travelling > 50 billion miles on them.

FURTHER READING

IT Governance Publishing (ITGP) is the world's leading publisher for governance and compliance. Our industry-leading pocket guides, books, training resources and toolkits are written by real-world practitioners and thought leaders. They are used globally by audiences of all levels, from students to C-suite executives.

Our high-quality publications cover all IT governance, risk and compliance frameworks and are available in a range of formats. This ensures our customers can access the information they need in the way they need it.

Our other publications about the NIS Directive include:

- *Network and Information Systems (NIS) Regulations - A pocket guide for digital service providers*

  www.itgovernancepublishing.co.uk/product/network-and-information-systems-nis-regulations-a-pocket-guide-for-digital-service-providers

- *A concise introduction to the NIS Directive - A pocket guide for digital service providers*

  www.itgovernancepublishing.co.uk/product/a-concise-introduction-to-the-nis-directive

For more information on ITGP and branded publishing services, and to view our full list of publications, visit *www.itgovernancepublishing.co.uk*.

To receive regular updates from ITGP, including information on new publications in your area(s) of interest, sign up for our newsletter at
www.itgovernancepublishing.co.uk/topic/newsletter.

Branded publishing

Through our branded publishing service, you can customise ITGP publications with your company's branding.

Find out more at
www.itgovernancepublishing.co.uk/topic/branded-publishing-services.

Related services

ITGP is part of GRC International Group, which offers a comprehensive range of complementary products and services to help organisations meet their objectives.

For a full range of resources on the NIS Directive visit *www.itgovernance.co.uk/shop/category/nis-regulations*.

Training services

The IT Governance training programme is built on our extensive practical experience designing and implementing management systems based on ISO standards, best practice and regulations.

Our courses help attendees develop practical skills and comply with contractual and regulatory requirements. They also support career development via recognised qualifications.

Learn more about our training courses and view the full course catalogue at *www.itgovernance.co.uk/training*.

Professional services and consultancy

We are a leading global consultancy of IT governance, risk management and compliance solutions. We advise businesses around the world on their most critical issues and present cost-saving and risk-reducing solutions based on international best practice and frameworks.

We offer a wide range of delivery methods to suit all budgets, timescales and preferred project approaches.

Find out how our consultancy services can help your organisation at *www.itgovernance.co.uk/consulting*.

Industry news

Want to stay up to date with the latest developments and resources in the IT governance and compliance market? Subscribe to our Daily Sentinel newsletter and we will send you mobile-friendly emails with fresh news and features about your preferred areas of interest, as well as unmissable offers and free resources to help you successfully start your projects. *www.itgovernance.co.uk/daily-sentinel*.

EU for product safety is Stephen Evans, The Mill Enterprise Hub, Stagreenan, Drogheda, Co. Louth, A92 CD3D, Ireland. (servicecentre@itgovernance.eu)

www.ingramcontent.com/pod-product-compliance
Lightning Source LLC
Chambersburg PA
CBHW070856070326
40690CB00009B/1871

* 9 7 8 1 7 8 7 7 8 0 5 2 1 *